# Disney PRINCESS
## Tea Parties

INSIGHT
EDITIONS

SAN RAFAEL · LOS ANGELES · LONDON

# Disney PRINCESS
## Tea Parties

By Sarah Walker Caron

INSIGHT
EDITIONS

San Rafael · Los Angeles · London

# Contents

## Chapter 3: Sweet Bakes 57

## Chapter 4: Tiny Sandwiches and Soups 83

## Chapter 5: Tea Party Sips 105

# Introduction

Snow White is resilient.
Cinderella is kind.
Aurora is a dreamer.
Ariel is curious.
Belle is inquisitive.
Jasmine is open-minded.
Pocahontas is intelligent.
Mulan is fearless.
Tiana is ambitious.
Rapunzel is creative.
Merida is strong.
Moana is bold.

From the first glimpse of Snow White in 1937, Disney Princesses have demonstrated caring and kindness, self-confidence and loyalty, and they've won the hearts and minds of generations. To be a Disney Princess is to overcome obstacles, outsmart villains, and embrace one's destiny, all while being a trustworthy and loyal friend.

From sweet tales featuring woodland creatures and beautiful melodic voices to bold stories of being fierce in the face of challenge, Disney Princess movies entertain while demonstrating guiding principles of favorable characteristics.

Hosting a tea party—especially one inspired by the admirable qualities of Disney Princesses—is an opportunity to celebrate a special occasion with family and friends. Celebrate your favorite Disney Princess by throwing a tea party drawing inspiration from the princesses and their lands.

In this cookbook, you'll find many delicious and fun recipes—some that might be new to you. All of the recipes are inspired by Disney Princesses, and many recipes are inspired by the cultures and people involved in the stories. Making and sharing the recipes is another way to discover similarities among people around the world.

# Plan a Perfect Disney Princess Tea Party

Princesses know how to celebrate! Whether it's setting off on a grand adventure to see floating lights for a birthday or hosting a grand opening for a dream-come-true restaurant, Disney Princess heroes are welcoming, kind, and thoughtful people who bring others together. Here's how you can bring some of that princess know-how to your special tea party.

## Step 1: Set a date, time, and place.

Check with parents to help set a day, hour, and location for your party. Allow enough time to plan, send invitations, decorate, and make or assemble food. Choose indoors for cool or wet weather; outdoors on warm and sunny days. Look around the location to determine whether it has enough space for your guests. Once those big decisions are made, it's time to send invitations.

## Step 2: Plan your menu.

Choose a mix of sweet and savory foods—pick at least one sweet and one savory recipe from this book. Add to your menu at least one familiar food that you know most people like—such as cut-up fresh veggies and fruits. Make the tea party extra special with a fancy, flavorful drink. See Chapter 5 (page 105) for lots of ideas.

## Step 3: Decorate and set the table.

A Disney Princess tea party is an elegant affair. Make your party space distinctive with a decorative cloth or paper table cover. Set out dainty teacups, plates, and silverware. Then place a vase of flowers (even wildflowers or silk flowers) in the center of the table.

## Step 4: Dress up.

Don't forget to ask your guests to dress as their favorite Disney Princess, or as a character from the theme you've chosen for the tea party. Dressing up and pretending to be a beloved Disney character during the party adds to the fun.

## Step 5: Plan at least one activity—maybe more.

What will you do during your tea party besides enjoy the delightful food and drink? A Disney Princess tea party is the perfect time to play princess trivia! Ask your guests trivia questions from your favorite Disney Princess movies. Or watch a movie together—perhaps it's even the one your food is themed after. And—if you're feeling crafty—do something creative. Why not set out supplies for making wands or tiaras and let your guests create something special to remember the day?

And above all, remember to have fun. That's the most important part of planning a perfect Disney Princess tea party!

# Tools of the Tea Party

Every prince or princess should be prepared with the right tools for their celebration and its food. These are a few of the special items you might need to make the recipes in this book (and serve them too!).

**Cookie cutters:** Recipes in this book call for cookie cutters in star, sun, heart, acorn, and flower shapes. A boxed set of assorted cookie cutters might have every shape necessary, or individual cutters in many shapes and sizes are widely available. Or different cutter shapes than those suggested in recipes, as long as they are similar size, can be substituted.

**Whisk:** There are many recipes that require a bit of whisking.

**Baking pans:** Depending on the recipe, a variety of pan shapes are sizes are useful—regular-size and mini muffin pans, individual-size fluted tube pans, full-size cake pans, and baking sheets.

**Pastry bags:** These are useful to pipe frosting on cupcakes and decorate tea cakes.

**Blender:** Particularly in the drinks section, this kitchen appliance is a must.

**Citrus juicer:** This device makes quick work of squeezing juice from fresh fruit. Many recipes call for freshly squeezed juice.

**Serving containers:** Petite glassware, small cups, and ramekins are useful and pretty to serve drinks, soups, and desserts.

**Serving trays:** Single and tiered trays make serving fancy foods easy and elegant.

**Teacups:** Although not absolutely required, fancy tea cups are fun to drink from, especially at a tea party.

# CHAPTER 1

# Little Bites

# Meeko Seed Crackers

Pocahontas's friend Meeko is a sly raccoon who absolutely adores food. These crispy homemade crackers, made with seeds that grow in the mid-Atlantic region where Pocahontas lived, would make Meeko's eyes glimmer and his mouth water. These crackers, good on their own, are also tasty served with cheese—definitely a choice that Meeko would approve.

## Makes about 30 crackers

1½ cups all-purpose flour

1 teaspoon sugar

1 teaspoon salt, plus extra for sprinkling

1 tablespoon sunflower seeds, chopped

1 tablespoon pepitas, chopped

3 tablespoons olive oil, divided

½ cup water

Preheat the oven to 400°F. Line a large baking sheet with parchment paper.

In a large bowl, sift together the flour, sugar, and salt. Stir in the sunflower seeds and pepitas.

Add 2 tablespoons of the olive oil and the water to the bowl; stir to combine. The dough will be crumbly. Use clean, floured hands to knead the dough until it forms a ball that holds together, 1 to 2 minutes.

Turn the dough out onto a floured cutting board. Use a rolling pin to roll the dough to ⅛-inch thickness.

Brush the dough with the remaining 1 tablespoon olive oil. Sprinkle with salt. Use a fork to prick holes all over the dough. Then cut the dough into shapes with 2-inch cookie cutters. Carefully transfer the shapes to the baking sheet.

Slide the baking sheet into the preheated oven and bake for 12 to 15 minutes, or until lightly golden. Transfer the crackers to a cooling rack and cool completely. Store the crackers in an airtight container for up to 1 week.

## Recipe Tip

For deliciously thin and crispy crackers, roll the dough to the suggested ⅛-inch thickness before cutting out. The thinner they are, the crispier they'll be.

# Merida Scottish Crumpets with Quick Raspberry Jam

Scottish crumpets are thin griddle cakes (like pancakes) that are spread with butter or jam, then rolled up to serve. They're hearty enough to fuel the Scottish adventures of Merida—and to satisfy appetites at tea time.

*Makes 12 crumpets and about 1 cup jam*

### For the raspberry jam

2 cups frozen raspberries

¼ cup granulated sugar

1 tablespoon cornstarch

### For the crumpets

1 large egg, separated

1 cup all-purpose flour

1 tablespoon sugar, plus more for sprinkling

Pinch salt

1 tablespoon melted butter, plus extra for greasing the griddle

1¼ cups milk

**To make the raspberry jam:** Add the raspberries, sugar, and cornstarch to a small saucepan. Heat over medium heat, stirring constantly, for 10 to 15 minutes. As the raspberries heat, they release juice and the mixture thickens. When the jam coats the spoon and leaves a wake when dragged through, it's done. Remove jam from the heat. Raspberry jam is delicious served warm or cool. To store leftover jam, refrigerate it in an airtight container up to 10 days.

**To make the crumpets:** Beat the egg yolk in a large bowl until frothing, about 3 minutes. Add the flour, sugar, and salt, and whisk to combine. Add the melted butter and milk; whisk well until fully incorporated, about 1 minute.

In a small bowl, beat the egg white to soft peaks, about 2 to 3 minutes. Add the egg white to the flour mixture in the large bowl and fold into the batter.

Heat a griddle over medium heat. Lightly grease griddle with butter. Drop the batter in ¼-cup rounds, spreading to about 5 inches in diameter. When tops are bubbly, flip the crumpets and cook until golden.

While crumpets are warm, spread with raspberry jam and roll up or fold in half. Sprinkle with sugar and serve immediately.

# Flora, Fauna, and Merryweather Fruit Wands

The three good fairies in *Sleeping Beauty* look after Briar Rose—that's their special name for Aurora—to keep her safe from Maleficent's evil curse. The fairies do love their magic wands, even if the wands can only be used for stirring tea—or making sweet fruit kebabs like these. The trick here is to slice the watermelon thick enough for the stars to stay on the skewers and not crack.

## Makes 8 wands and about 1/2 cup yogurt dip

### For the fruit kebabs

1 mini watermelon

Assorted fruit such as grapes, small strawberries, and blueberries

Skewers

### For the yogurt dip

½ cup vanilla yogurt

1 teaspoon minced fresh mint

Zest of 1 lime

**To make the fruit kebabs:** Place the watermelon on a cutting board and slice it through the center. Place one of the cut ends on the cutting board and careful cut away all the rind. Slice the watermelon into ¾-inch-thick slices. Use a 3- to 4-inch star-shape cookie cutter to cut out 8 stars.

One kebab at a time, thread the grapes, strawberries, and blueberries onto a skewer, using 6 to 8 pieces of fruit. Leave half of the skewer free for a handle, and leave enough room at the sharp end for the watermelon stars.

Carefully thread the watermelon stars onto the end of each skewer.

**To make the yogurt dip:** In a small bowl, stir together the yogurt, mint, and lime zest. Serve with the fruit kebabs for dipping.

## Recipe Tip

Cube the remaining watermelon and chill it in an airtight container for snacking.

# Whistle While You Wurst Lettuce Wraps

Wursts—German sausages—are a favorite food that comes in many varieties. In these fun lettuce wraps, diced bratwurst is combined with veggies and apples to create a sweet-savory filling that would please even the grumpiest of mine workers.

## Makes 12 lettuce wraps

1 tablespoon olive oil

1 apple, diced (about 1 cup)

½ cup diced red onion

⅓ cup shredded carrot

Salt and freshly ground black pepper

½ pound precooked bratwurst, diced

1 head butter lettuce

2 scallions, thinly sliced

Heat the olive oil in a large skillet over medium heat. Add the apple, onion, and carrot to the skillet, and season with salt and pepper. Cook, stirring occasionally, for 5 to 7 minutes, or until softened.

Add the bratwurst to the skillet and stir to combine. Cook, stirring, for 3 to 4 minutes, or until heated through. Remove the skillet from the heat.

Divide the bratwurst mixture among 12 lettuce leaf "cups." Top the lettuce wrap with the sliced scallions.

# Mulan Pork and Vegetable Dumplings

In China during Lunar New Year celebrations, crescent-shape dumplings are served to represent hopes for a prosperous year ahead. Dumplings are served other times of the year as well, and in a variety of ways. This recipe for pork and vegetable dumplings was inspired by the dumplings shared by Mulan's family on the evening before Mulan leaves home—determined to honor and protect her family.

### Makes about 25 dumplings

2 cups shredded napa cabbage (about ⅛ of a medium head)

½ teaspoon salt

½ pound ground pork

¼ cup thinly sliced scallions

¼ cup minced fresh cilantro

2 teaspoons soy sauce, plus more for serving

1½ teaspoons grated fresh ginger

1 clove garlic, minced

1½ teaspoons sesame oil

1 large egg, whisked

½ (12-ounce) package round dumpling wrappers

1 tablespoon canola oil

Place the cabbage in a colander set in the sink. Toss cabbage with the salt, then let it stand for 5 to 10 minutes. Press the cabbage to squeeze out as much water as you can.

Transfer the squeezed cabbage to a large bowl. Add the ground pork, scallions, cilantro, soy sauce, ginger, garlic, sesame oil, and egg. Use clean hands to combine thoroughly.

Line a baking sheet with parchment paper.

Open the dumpling wrappers, keeping wrappers well covered while working with one at a time (wrappers dry out quickly when exposed to air).

For each dumpling, place one wrapper on a work surface. Spoon a heaping teaspoon of filling in the center. Dampen wrapper edges with a bit of water, then fold wrapper in half diagonally around filling. Pleat and press edges together firmly to seal.

Add canola oil to a large skillet and heat over high heat. Carefully arrange the dumplings in the skillet, pleated edge up, allowing space between each. Cook the dumplings about 2 minutes, or until the bottoms are golden. Carefully add ½ cup water to the skillet then cover immediately. Reduce the heat to low and cook 4 to 6 minutes, or until the dumplings are softened and the filling is cooked through. Serve with additional soy sauce.

# Jasmine Jeweled Yogurt Parfaits

Princess Jasmine is compassionate, caring, strong, and independent. She doesn't want anyone else to decide her future. These delicious yogurt parfaits remind us of her: Impressive with layers of yogurt, nuts, and colorful fruit, but also sweet and comforting—a lovely dish to enjoy at your next tea party.

### Makes four 8-ounce parfaits

2 cups plain yogurt

¼ to ⅓ cup honey

1 teaspoon vanilla extract

1 teaspoon cinnamon

¼ cup sliced almonds

¼ cup pomegranate arils

¼ cup chopped pistachios

¼ cup dried cranberries

In a mixing bowl, whisk the yogurt, honey, vanilla, and cinnamon.

In each of four half-pint Mason jars or bowls, layer 2 tablespoons of the yogurt mixture, 1 tablespoon almonds, 2 tablespoons yogurt, 1 tablespoon pomegranate arils, 2 tablespoons yogurt, 1 tablespoon chopped pistachios, 2 tablespoons yogurt, and 1 tablespoon dried cranberries.

Serve immediately, or cover and chill until ready to serve.

# Rapunzel Trusty Cast-Iron Skillet Potato Pancakes with Applesauce

Rapunzel acts quickly with her trusty cast-iron skillet as Flynn Rider intrudes upon her secluded tower. As it happens, a cast-iron skillet is handy for so much more than self-defense. It can be used to cook potato pancakes that are crunchy on the outside and tender on the inside. Served with a dollop of cool applesauce, these pancakes are fireworks of flavor.

*Makes about 12 potato pancakes and 1 cup applesauce*

### For the applesauce

3 apples, peeled and cut into chunks

¼ cup water

2 tablespoons lemon juice

¼ teaspoon ground cinnamon

### For the potato pancakes

1 pound russet potatoes, peeled and coarsely grated

1 small onion, finely chopped

2 tablespoons all-purpose flour

1 teaspoon kosher salt

½ teaspoon black pepper

1 large egg, lightly beaten

Vegetable oil

**To make the applesauce:** In a small saucepan, combine the apples, water, lemon juice, and ground cinnamon. Stir well to combine. Cook, covered, over medium heat for 10 to 15 minutes, or until the apples are very soft. If the water evaporates during cooking, add ¼ cup water. Remove the saucepan from the heat. Use a potato masher to mash the apples. Stir well. Serve the applesauce warm over pancakes. Cover and refrigerate any remaining applesauce up to 3 days.

Set the potatoes and onion in a colander in the sink to drain for 10 minutes. Cover potatoes and onion with paper towels, then press with your hands to extract as much liquid as possible.

Transfer the vegetables to a large mixing bowl. Add the flour, salt, and pepper. Stir to combine. Add the egg and stir to combine.

Line a plate with paper towels; set aside. Add enough vegetable oil to a large skillet to cover the bottom. Heat the skillet over medium-high. When the oil is hot, drop ¼-cup portions of potato mixture into the skillet. Press the rounds lightly with a spatula to flatten. Cook for 4 to 5 minutes per side, or until undersides of pancakes are golden. Transfer cooked pancakes to prepared plate while cooking remaining pancakes. Serve pancakes while warm with warm applesauce.

# Pocahontas Fried Squash Patties

Along the coast of Virginia, where Pocahontas lived during the 17th century, corn and squash were primary sources of food. In this recipe, squash is the featured ingredient in delicious fried patties to serve alongside tea.

## Makes about 12 patties

- 1 cup mashed butternut squash
- ½ cup all-purpose flour
- 1 shallot, minced
- 1 large egg, lightly beaten
- ¼ teaspoon salt
- ¼ teaspoon freshly ground black pepper
- ½ teaspoon dried thyme
- Vegetable oil
- Plain Greek yogurt and sliced green onions, for garnish

Line a plate with paper towels; set aside. In a large bowl, stir together the butternut squash, flour, shallot, egg, salt, pepper, and thyme.

Heat 1 to 2 tablespoons of vegetable oil in a large skillet over medium heat. When the oil is hot, drop ¼-cup portions of squash mixture into the skillet, allowing space for patties to expand as they cook. Cook 4 to 5 minutes per side, or until golden brown, turning once halfway through cooking.

Transfer cooked patties to the prepared plate, and cover to keep warm while cooking remaining patties.

Serve immediately topped with yogurt and sliced green onions.

## Recipe Tip

Refrigerated or frozen peeled squash, available in most grocery stores, is quick and easy to heat and mash. Seasonal fresh squash would need to be peeled, seeded, cubed, cooked, and mashed for this recipe. Canned pumpkin would make a fair substitute for squash in this recipe.

# Seven Dwarfs Chicken Schnitzel Bites

In the forest, after being spared by the Queen's Huntsman, Snow White takes up residence with the Seven Dwarfs and lovingly prepares meals to serve these hard working miners. After a full day, the Dwarfs would surely look forward to a meal like schnitzel—thinly pounded chicken that's breaded and fried crispy—especially with a dash of freshly squeezed lemon juice.

## *Makes about 16 schnitzel bites*

1 pound chicken breasts (about 2 breasts)

1 cup all-purpose flour

1 teaspoon salt, plus a pinch

1 teaspoon black pepper, plus a pinch

1 large egg

¼ teaspoon dry mustard

1 cup panko bread crumbs

¼ cup canola oil

1 tablespoon chopped fresh parsley

1 lemon, cut into 8 wedges

Pound each chicken breast to ¼-inch thickness. Cut each breast into 8 pieces.

Sift the flour, the 1 teaspoon salt, and the 1 teaspoon pepper onto a plate.

Combine the egg, mustard, and a pinch each of salt and pepper in a small bowl; whisk thoroughly to combine.

Place the bread crumbs on a second plate.

Coat each piece of chicken first in flour, then in the egg mixture, then in bread crumbs. Set each piece on a plate.

Line a plate with paper towels; set aside. Heat the oil in a large skillet over medium heat. Add the chicken in a single layer to the pan. Cook for 2 to 3 minutes, turn, and cook another 2 to 3 minutes, or until golden and cooked through. Transfer to the towel-lined plate.

Sprinkle the chicken with parsley and serve with lemon wedges. Direct guests to squeeze the lemon onto the schnitzel.

# Opening Night Meatballs

Tiana works hard to live her dream of opening her own restaurant in New Orleans. The dream is one that she shared with her father, who believed that food brings people together. These sweet and savory meatballs are sure to bring people together—for the opening of Tiana's Palace or for a fun tea party with special guests.

## Makes 6 to 8 servings

1 pound ground beef (85% lean)

¾ cup panko bread crumbs

1 teaspoon paprika

1 teaspoon packed light brown sugar

1 teaspoon garlic powder

1 teaspoon salt

½ teaspoon black pepper

½ cup chili sauce

½ cup apricot preserves

1 tablespoon soy sauce

1 scallion, thinly sliced

Preheat the oven to 375°F. Line a baking sheet with parchment paper.

In a large bowl, combine the ground beef, bread crumbs, paprika, brown sugar, garlic powder, salt, and pepper with your hands.

Form the beef mixture into 1-inch meatballs. Place meatballs ½ inch apart on the prepared baking sheet. Bake the meatballs 16 to 20 minutes, or until cooked through.

In a small saucepan over medium heat, combine the chili sauce, apricot preserves, and soy sauce, stirring constantly until bubbling, 3 to 4 minutes. Remove from heat.

In a large bowl, carefully coat the meatballs with sauce. Arrange saucy meatballs on a platter, then sprinkle with the sliced scallion. To serve, provide wooden picks to spear meatballs.

# CHAPTER 2

# Savory Bakes

# Cave of Wonders Cardamom Breadsticks

Brimming with riches, jewels, and magical items—including the Genie's magic lamp—the Cave of Wonders is a pretty special place. These soft, pillowy breadsticks are pretty special too. Flavored with cardamom, a spice popular in Middle Eastern cooking, they are delightful served with a cup of warm tea.

## Makes 20 breadsticks

1⅓ cups warm water

1½ teaspoons active dry yeast

2 tablespoons sugar

3 cups all-purpose flour

1 teaspoon salt

1 teaspoon cardamom

1 tablespoon unsalted butter, melted

Coarse salt, for sprinkling

In a large bowl, combine the water, yeast, and sugar; let stand for 10 minutes or until the yeast foams. Stir the yeast mixture if specks of yeast appear not yet moistened. Add 1½ cups of the flour, the salt, and cardamom to the bowl, then stir to combine. Add the remaining 1½ cups of flour and stir to combine. The dough will be sticky and should pull away from the sides of the bowl. With floured hands, knead dough until smooth, 4 to 5 minutes.

Transfer the dough to an extra-large greased bowl. Cover the bowl with a towel. Let the dough rise at least 90 minutes, or until doubled in size.

Line a baking sheet with parchment paper. Punch dough down. Evenly divide dough into 20 portions. Roll each portion into a ¾-inch-diameter stick about 8 to 10 inches long. Space breadsticks on prepared baking sheet, allowing 1 inch between each stick. (If necessary, use two baking sheets.) Cover breadsticks with a damp towel and let rise for 1 hour.

Preheat the oven to 425°F. Brush the breadsticks with the melted butter and sprinkle with coarse salt. Bake for 10 to 12 minutes, or until golden. Remove the breadsticks from the oven, and transfer to a wire rack to cool slightly.

# Enchanted Pizza Roses

The Beast keeps the enchanted rose under a glass dome, hidden in a wing of his castle where no one is allowed. Chances are you won't hide these pizza roses. They're a yummy combo of puff pastry, marinara sauce, melty cheese, and pepperoni that you'll be eager to share with tea party friends.

## Makes 8 pizza roses

Cooking oil spray, for greasing

1 sheet frozen puff pastry, thawed completely

½ cup marinara sauce

½ cup mozzarella cheese

12 slices deli pepperoni, cut in half

Preheat the oven to 400°F. Grease 8 cups of a standard muffin tin with cooking oil spray.

Spread the puff pastry on a cutting board. Using a pizza cutter, cut the pastry into 8 strips. Separate the strips. Spread some of the marinara sauce onto each of the strips and sprinkle with the cheese, dividing evenly among each strip. On each pastry strip, layer and overlap 3 pepperoni halves, with cut edges at center of pastry and rounded edges extending beyond strip edges. Fold the ends of the strips over pepperoni, then roll the pastry to resemble roses.

Place the pizza roses in muffin cups, rounded pepperoni edges to the top.

Bake for 20 to 25 minutes, or until golden brown. Remove the pizza roses from the oven, and cool on a wire rack about 5 minutes. Remove from cups and serve warm.

# Tiana Roasted Cajun Shrimp Cocktail

Tiana lives in New Orleans, in well-known Cajun country where cuisine is spicy hot and music is soulful and dreamy. This bold shrimp cocktail would be right at home in Tiana's restaurant, where heat-loving dreamers gather for good times.

## Makes 6 to 8 servings

1 pound large shrimp, peeled and deveined with tails on

1 tablespoon olive oil

1 tablespoon Cajun seasoning

1 tablespoon unsalted butter

Cocktail sauce or tartar sauce, for serving

In a large bowl, toss together the shrimp, olive oil, and Cajun seasoning until the shrimp are well-coated.

Melt the butter in a large skillet over medium heat. Add the shrimp. Cook for 3 to 5 minutes, flipping once, until the shrimp are opaque in color and lightly golden.

Serve the shrimp with cocktail sauce or tartar sauce for dipping.

## Recipe Tip

For a pretty presentation, set a small dish or glass of cocktail sauce in a large bowl, then arrange shrimp in the bowl around the sauce. Provide wooden picks to spear the shrimp.

# Belle Provincial Vegetable Tarts

Strong, ambitious, and brilliant, Belle loves to read—a trait that sets her apart from some of the other French villagers. These vegetable tarts are set apart too, flavored with herbes de Provence—a blend of basil, rosemary, thyme, savory, marjoram, oregano, and lavender that's common in French cuisine.

## Makes 8 tarts

1 frozen puff pastry sheet, thawed

Eight ¼-inch slices fresh zucchini (about half a small zucchini)

Eight ¼-inch slices plum tomatoes (about 1½ tomatoes)

Eight ¼-inch slices shallot (about 1 large shallot)

1 tablespoon olive oil

1 teaspoon herbes de Provence

½ teaspoon salt

¼ teaspoon black pepper

Preheat the oven to 375°F.

Line a baking sheet with parchment paper. Unfold the puff pastry sheet and cut into 8 rectangles. For best results, cut it in half the long way and then cut 4 even strips the short way. Place them on the prepared baking sheet, not touching.

On the center of each puff pastry piece, place one slice of zucchini, one slice of tomato, and one slice of shallot, overlapping slightly.

In a small bowl, stir together the olive oil, herbes de Provence, salt, and pepper. Drizzle the mixture onto the vegetables, dividing evenly among the 8 tarts.

Bake for 28 to 30 minutes, or until the pastry is golden brown and puffed. Serve warm.

# Ariel Roasted Tomato Mini Pies

Ariel saves the dashing Prince Eric from drowning, dazzling him with her melodic voice. Meanwhile, Eric captures her heart as well. You, too, can be someone who captures hearts—by serving flavorful tomato pie hearts at a tea party.

## Makes 16 mini pies

- 1 (14.1-ounce) box refrigerated pie crusts, at room temperature (2 crusts)
- 1 cup chopped grape tomatoes
- 2 cloves garlic, minced
- 1 teaspoon cornstarch
- Salt and black pepper
- 1 tablespoon chopped fresh basil

Preheat the oven to 375°F. Line a large baking sheet with parchment paper.

Unroll the pie crusts on a cutting board. Use a 3-inch heart-shape cookie cutter to cut out 8 hearts from each crust. Arrange cutouts, spacing closely without touching, on prepared baking sheet.

In a medium bowl, stir together the tomatoes, garlic, cornstarch, and salt and pepper to taste. Spoon some of the mixture onto the center of each heart, leaving edges uncovered.

Bake for 13 to 15 minutes, or until the pie crust is golden. Remove the hearts from the oven, and carefully transfer them to a serving plate. Sprinkle with fresh basil to serve.

# Merida Savory Almond Bear Claw Biscuits

Basic baking powder biscuits get a punch of flavor and paw-like flair in this almond-scented recipe. As a tribute to the moment when Merida reaches for her mother's paw and is saved from the claws of Mor'du, these cute biscuits will be a tea time highlight.

## Makes 8 biscuits

1 cup all-purpose flour

½ teaspoon salt

2 teaspoons baking powder

2 tablespoons cold unsalted butter, cut into 8 pieces

¼ cup plus 2 tablespoons milk

1 teaspoon almond extract

40 almond slices

1 egg white, beaten

Preheat the oven to 350°F. Line a large baking sheet with parchment paper.

In a large bowl, sift together the flour, salt, and baking powder. Add the butter to the bowl. Using a pastry cutter or two knives, cut the butter into the flour mixture until it resembles coarse crumbs. Add the milk and almond extract, and stir to mix. The dough will be crumbly.

Turn the dough out onto a floured cutting board. Using clean, floured hands, knead the dough lightly until a cohesive ball forms. Use a floured rolling pin to roll the dough to ½-inch thickness.

Cut the dough into 2-inch rounds with a biscuit cutter, gathering and rerolling dough to form a total of 8 biscuits.

Place the biscuits on the prepared baking sheet. Press 5 almond slices into the top edge of each biscuit, forming the "bear nails." Brush the biscuits with the egg white. Bake for 15 to 17 minutes, until golden brown. Enjoy hot from the oven.

Extra biscuits can be stored at room temperature in an airtight container up to 2 days.

# Heart of Te Fiti Spinach-Artichoke-Mozzarella Pinwheels

Moana sails away on a voyage to return the Heart of TeFiti to its rightful place and restore balance to the world. These little pinwheels, filled with spinach, artichokes, and mozzarella, are meant to be symbols of the mythical heart.

## Makes 8 pinwheels

1 sheet puff pastry, thawed

½ cup ricotta cheese

1 cup baby spinach

2 cloves garlic, minced

¼ teaspoon salt

⅛ teaspoon black pepper

½ cup chopped canned artichoke hearts, drained well

1 cup shredded mozzarella cheese

Preheat the oven to 350°F. Line a large baking sheet with parchment paper.

Lay the puff pastry on a lightly floured cutting board.

In the bowl of a food processor or blender, combine the ricotta cheese, spinach, garlic, salt, and pepper. Process until well combined (the mixture should be green). Spread the ricotta mixture on the puff pastry. Sprinkle the pastry and ricotta mixture with the artichoke hearts and mozzarella cheese, then roll the pastry into a log. Place the log in the freezer for 20 to 30 minutes to firm up.

Use a sharp knife to cut the rolled-up pastry into ¾-inch pieces. Place each slice on the baking sheet, gently reshaping into a round if necessary.

Bake for 22 to 24 minutes, or until the tops are golden brown. Remove the pinwheels from the oven and cool on a wire rack for 10 minutes before transferring to a serving platter. Enjoy warm.

# Gus-Gus Cheddar Puffs

Aww, Gus-Gus! This friendly mouse is as sweet and silly as they come—and he loves food. These cheese gougeres—delicate, savory French cheese puffs—are sure to charm tea party guests as much as they would attract Gus-Gus.

*Makes about 20 puffs*

½ cup unsalted butter

1 cup water

½ teaspoon salt

1 cup all-purpose flour

4 large eggs

1 cup shredded sharp cheddar cheese

1 teaspoon herbes de Provence (thyme can be substituted)

Preheat the oven to 425°F. Line a baking sheet with parchment paper.

In a medium saucepan, combine the butter, water, and salt. Bring the mixture to a boil over high heat. As soon as it boils, add the flour and reduce the heat to medium. Stir vigorously with a wooden spoon. The dough will begin to pull away from the side of the pan (this happens very quickly—within a minute or two). That's your cue to remove the pan from the heat. Let cool for 5 minutes.

Once cooled, add the eggs one at a time to the dough, stirring vigorously with the wooden spoon after each addition. Continue until all eggs have been added. The dough will become creamy. Add the cheese and herbes de Provence, stirring vigorously to combine.

Drop the dough in 1-tablespoon mounds, spacing mounds 1 inch apart, onto the baking sheet. (Or use a medium-size cookie scoop.)

Bake for 10 minutes. Reduce the heat to 325°F and bake an additional 15 to 20 minutes, or until puffed and golden. Let cool for 10 minutes before eating.

Serve the puffs warm. Cover and refrigerate remaining puffs up to 5 days. Reheat stored puffs at 350°F for 8 to 10 minutes.

# Once Upon a Dream Ham-and-Cheddar Quiche Bites

Before Aurora learns she is a princess (and not actually named Briar Rose), she shares a moment with Prince Phillip in the woods where they sing about walking with each other once upon a dream. You might feel the same way when you taste these familiar ham-and-cheese quiche bites. A delicate round of pie crust holds airy eggs, robust cheese, and ham in this savory tea time snack.

## Makes about 22 quiche bites

Nonstick baking spray

1 refrigerated rolled unbaked pie crust

3 large eggs

⅓ cup milk

Pinch salt and freshly ground black pepper

½ cup small-diced ham

¼ cup shredded sharp cheddar cheese

Preheat the oven to 375°F. Spray the cups of mini muffin pans with nonstick baking spray.

With a 2½-inch biscuit cutter, cut rounds from the pie crust, gathering and rerolling pastry scraps to cut as many rounds as possible. Fold each round in quarters, fit into a muffin cup, and gently press in place.

In a medium bowl, whisk together the eggs, milk, salt, and pepper until fully combined, about 1 minute. Divide the egg mixture evenly among the prepared pie crusts. Drop in the ham pieces and top with the cheese, again dividing evenly among muffin cups. Bake for 25 to 27 minutes, or until cooked through and lightly golden on top.

Remove the quiche bites from the oven, and cool on a wire rack for 5 minutes. Remove from muffin cups and serve warm.

The quiche bites can be stored in a covered container in the refrigerator for up to 4 days. Reheat in the microwave before serving.

### Recipe Tip

To easily remove quiche bites from cups, carefully run a knife gently around edges, then lift out.

# I Want More Savory Mushroom Bread Pudding

Ariel has gadgets and gizmos aplenty, and who's-its and what's-its galore. This bread pudding has something in common with those collections, except it's tasty: Tender bread cubes are surrounded with mushrooms and cheese aplenty.

## Makes 6 to 8 servings

½ loaf Italian bread, cut into ½-inch cubes (about 4 cups)

1 tablespoon olive oil

1 medium onion, diced

Salt and black pepper

2 garlic cloves, minced

8 ounces mushrooms, chopped

1 teaspoon dried thyme

1 teaspoon dried marjoram

2 large eggs

¾ cup milk

½ cup vegetable stock

1 cup shredded Gruyère cheese

Preheat the oven to 350°F. Arrange the bread cubes on a baking sheet and bake for 8 to 10 minutes, or until dry but not browned. Set aside. Leave the oven set to 350°F.

Heat the olive oil in a large skillet set over medium heat. Add the onion and season lightly with salt and pepper. Cook, stirring occasionally, for 10 to 12 minutes, or until very soft and golden. Add the garlic and mushrooms. Season with the thyme, marjoram, and a pinch of salt and pepper. Cook, stirring occasionally, about 10 minutes, until the mushrooms are browned. Remove the skillet from the heat.

In a large bowl, whisk together the eggs, milk, and stock. Stir in the cheese and dried bread cubes. Let stand for 5 minutes. Stir in the mushroom mixture. Pour the mixture into an 8-inch square casserole dish. Bake for 40 to 45 minutes, or until golden brown and set.

Cool on a wire rack for 5 minutes. Serve warm.

# CHAPTER 3

# Sweet Bakes

# Colors of the Wind Mini Cakes

Pocahontas certainly sees the beauty, brilliance, and liveliness of the world around her. She even sings about all she sees in the song "Colors of the Wind." These delicate little cakes are meant to remind guests of Pocahontas and her vivid, bright song.

### Makes 12 mini cakes

#### For the cakes

Softened butter, for greasing the pan

1 cup all-purpose flour, plus more for dusting

½ cup sugar

1 teaspoon baking soda

1 teaspoon baking powder

½ teaspoon salt

1 large egg

½ cup milk

¼ cup unsalted butter, melted

1 teaspoon vanilla extract

#### For the glaze

1 cup confectioners' sugar

½ teaspoon vanilla extract

1 to 2 tablespoons milk

Food coloring

**To make the cakes:** Preheat the oven to 350°F. Grease the cups of a 12-cavity mini fluted cake mold with softened butter and dust with flour.

In a medium bowl, sift together the 1 cup flour, the sugar, baking soda, baking powder, and salt.

In a large bowl, whisk together the egg, milk, the melted butter, and vanilla until well combined. Add the flour mixture and stir just until combined. Divide the batter evenly among the cake molds. Tap the pan gently to settle batter and release excess air.

Bake for 16 to 18 minutes, or until golden.

Remove cakes from oven. Cool in pan on a wire rack for 10 minutes. Remove cakes from pan and cool completely on wire rack.

**To make the glaze:** Line a baking sheet with waxed paper. Place the wire rack with the cakes on the baking sheet.

In a medium bowl, combine the confectioners' sugar, vanilla, and 1 tablespoon of milk; stir until combined and a thick drizzling consistency. Divide the icing among four bowls. Color each a different color. If icing becomes thick, add a few drops of milk and stir well. Drizzle each color icing over mini cakes.

# Witch Spell Cakes

When fierce Merida is caught between her mother's wish for her to make a smart marriage match and her own heart's desire to be her own person, she accepts help from a witch—in the form of a spell cake to change her mother's mind. Alas, all is not as it seems. Merida's mother is transformed into a bear. No such worry with these spell cakes—also known as cherry pies—because they're all treat and no trick.

## Makes about 20 mini pies

2 cups frozen pitted cherries

½ cup sugar

2 tablespoons cornstarch

1 (14.1-ounce) box refrigerated pie crusts, at room temperature (2 crusts)

In a small saucepan over medium heat, combine the cherries, sugar, and cornstarch. Cook, stirring constantly, for 8 to 10 minutes, or until the cherries defrost, releasing their juices, and the mixture thickens. Remove the saucepan from the heat and cool for 30 minutes.

Preheat the oven to 375°F.

Unroll the pie crusts onto a cutting board. Use a round 3-inch cookie or biscuit cutter to cut rounds from the dough. Place the rounds into the cups of a mini muffin pan. Gather and reroll scraps as necessary to get additional rounds.

Divide the cherry mixture evenly among the mini pie crusts. Bake for 20 to 25 minutes, or until the crust is golden and the cherry filling has puffed. Cool on a wire rack before serving.

# Bibbidi-Bobbidi Blueberry-Lemon Scones

With a flourish of her wand and a few magic words, Cinderella's Fairy Godmother transforms Cinderella into an elegant belle of the ball. Those same magic words (and a little bit of baking) will transform basic ingredients into magical lemon-blueberry scones.

## Makes 16 mini scones

1¾ cups all-purpose flour

1 teaspoon baking powder

2 tablespoons sugar

½ teaspoon salt

Zest and juice of 1 lemon, separated

¼ cup cold unsalted butter, cut into pieces

⅔ cup frozen wild blueberries

2 large eggs, beaten

⅓ cup buttermilk

½ cup confectioners' sugar

Preheat the oven to 350°F. Line a baking sheet with parchment paper.

In a large bowl, sift together the flour, baking powder, sugar, salt, and lemon zest. With a pastry blender or two knives, cut cold butter into flour mixture. Stir in the blueberries.

Make a well in the center of the flour mixture and add the beaten eggs and buttermilk. Fold together just until moistened. The dough will be crumbly.

Turn the dough out onto a floured cutting board. Pat gently, pressing the dough together while forming two ¾-inch-thick circles. Use a pizza cutter to cut each circle into 8 wedges.

Transfer the wedges to the prepared baking sheet. Bake for 20 to 24 minutes, or until just beginning to turn golden on the top. Remove the scones from the oven. Cool for 10 minutes.

In a small bowl, stir together the confectioners' sugar and 2 to 3 teaspoons of lemon juice until well combined. The glaze should drizzle easily but not be too thin. Spoon the glaze over the scones.

Serve immediately. Once glazed, the scones don't save well.

## Recipe Tip

The scones can be made up to 3 days ahead and stored, unglazed, in an airtight container at room temperature. Glaze the scones right before serving.

# Under the Seashell Cinnamon-Pear Tarts

Sebastian likes things best under the sea, where life is sweet and he has no troubles. These tarts are certainly no trouble to whip up. They hide a buttery brown sugar filling under a layer of sweet pears, making them a delightful tea-party-time treat.

## Makes 4 tarts

1 sheet frozen puff pastry, at room temperature

2 tablespoons packed dark brown sugar

2 tablespoons unsalted butter, softened

⅛ teaspoon salt

1¼ teaspoons cinnamon, divided

2 pears, peeled, halved, and cored

2 teaspoons granulated sugar

Preheat the oven to 400°F. Line a baking sheet with parchment paper.

Spread the puff pastry on a floured cutting board. Use a 4-inch flower-shape cookie cutter to cut the dough into 4 rounds. Arrange the cut dough on the baking sheet.

In a small bowl, stir together the brown sugar, butter, salt, and 1 teaspoon of the cinnamon. Divide the mixture evenly among the flowers, mounding in the center.

Cut the pears into ⅛-inch slices, leaving the stem end attached. Spread the cut ends of pears out slightly as you place them cored-side down on the flowers, covering the butter mixture. In a small bowl, stir together the granulated sugar and remaining ¼ teaspoon cinnamon. Sprinkle cinnamon-sugar mixture over the pears.

Bake for 18 to 20 minutes, or until the puff pastry is browned. Remove the tarts from the oven. Cool for 10 minutes. Serve warm.

# Moana Edge of the Water Cupcakes

From a young age, Moana is called to the ocean, dazzled by the glimmering light and beckoned by gentle waves. As the water offers gifts and invites Moana closer, she dreams of paddling beyond the reef—though her father prohibits her from actually paddling out. These vanilla cupcakes, with pretty vanilla frosting decorations, suggest Moana's connection to the water's edge.

## Makes 10 cupcakes

### For the cupcakes

1 cup all-purpose flour

½ cup sugar

1 teaspoon baking soda

1 teaspoon baking powder

½ teaspoon salt

1 large egg

½ cup milk

¼ cup canola oil

1 teaspoon vanilla extract

2 tablespoons blue sprinkles

### For the frosting

½ cup unsalted butter, softened

1½ cup confectioners' sugar

1 teaspoon vanilla extract

1 tablespoon milk

Blue food coloring

Graham crackers, crushed

**To make the cupcakes:** Preheat the oven to 375°F. Line 10 muffin cups with liners.

In a large bowl, sift together the flour, sugar, baking soda, baking powder, and salt.

In a small bowl, whisk together the egg, milk, oil, and vanilla until smooth. Add the egg mixture to the flour mixture and stir to combine. Stir in the sprinkles. Divide the batter evenly among the 10 muffin cups. Bake for 15 to 18 minutes, or until golden (a toothpick inserted into the center of the cupcakes should come out clean). Cool the cupcakes completely on a wire rack.

**To make the frosting:** Once the cupcakes are cooled, in a large bowl combine the butter, confectioners' sugar, and vanilla. Use a handheld mixer (or a stand mixer) to mix slowly together on the lowest speed. Once the ingredients are mostly incorporated, beat on high until smooth. Add the milk and beat again to combine.

Lightly frost the cupcakes using no more than half of the frosting. Place the crushed graham crackers in a shallow bowl. Then dip half of each cupcake top into the crushed graham crackers.

Take the remaining frosting and remove about half to a second bowl. Use the blue food coloring to tint one half of the frosting.

Fit an empty 12-inch pastry bag with a star tip. Fill two 12-inch pastry bags separately with the blue and white frosting, being careful not to overfill bags. Cut off the tips of both bags and place both bags inside the prepared pastry bag. Twist and close the tops of all of the bags.

Pipe waves of blue and white onto each of the cupcakes (on the side without graham crackers).

# Nakoma Corn Cookies

While harvesting corn in the fields—far from any listening ears—Pocahontas and her best friend, Nakoma, talk freely about the future of Pocahontas. As a tribute to Pocahontas and a treat to share with your closest friends, these buttery, lightly sweet cookies are made with cornmeal.

## Makes about 2 dozen cookies

- ¾ cup unsalted butter, at room temperature
- ½ cup granulated sugar
- ¼ cup packed light brown sugar
- 1 large egg
- 1 teaspoon vanilla extract
- ¼ cup cornmeal
- 1 teaspoon baking powder
- ½ teaspoon salt
- 1½ cups all-purpose flour

Preheat the oven to 350°F. Line a large baking sheet with parchment paper.

In a large bowl (or the bowl of a stand mixer), add the butter, granulated sugar, and brown sugar. Beat until creamy using a hand mixer (or a stand mixer fitted with the paddle attachment), about 2 minutes. Add the egg and vanilla, and mix well for about 1 minute.

In a medium bowl, sift together the cornmeal, baking powder, salt, and flour. With the mixer running on low, add the dry ingredients to the wet ingredients a little at a time until completely mixed. Use a medium cookie scoop (or two spoons) to drop in about 1-tablespoon rounds onto the baking sheet, leaving about 1 inch between each cookie.

Bake for 13 to 16 minutes, or until lightly browned.

Transfer cookies to a wire rack to cool. They can be stored in an airtight container at room temperature for up to 5 days.

# Mulan Blossom Tea Cakes

When Mulan's father sits with her outside after the disastrous meeting with the village matchmaker, he points out the beautiful blossoms that surround them—and one that isn't quite blooming yet. The flower that blooms later than the rest, he says, might just turn out to be the most beautiful of all. These beautiful little cakes are dense, lightly sweetened, fragrant, and decorated with blossoms, making them perfect for eating with your favorite tea.

## Makes about 24 mini tea cakes

### For the cakes

½ cup canola oil

1 cup granulated sugar

2 large eggs

1 teaspoon vanilla extract

1 teaspoon orange blossom water

⅓ cup milk

2 cups all-purpose flour

1 tablespoon baking powder

½ teaspoon salt

### For the icing

1 cup confectioners' sugar

1 tablespoon water

½ teaspoon orange blossom water or vanilla extract

Red and yellow food coloring

**To make the cakes:** Preheat the oven to 350°F. Line a 24-cup mini muffin pan with liners.

In a large bowl. whisk together the oil, sugar, eggs, vanilla, orange blossom water, and milk until well combined.

In a medium bowl, sift together the flour, baking powder, and salt. Add the flour mixture to the oil mixture and fold together until well combined. Divide the batter evenly among the muffin cups, being careful not to overfill. Bake 15 to 18 minutes, or until golden and cooked through. Remove from the oven and cool completely.

**To make the icing:** Stir together confectioners' sugar, water, and orange blossom water in a small bowl. Tint about 3 tablespoons of the icing light red. Tint the remaining icing light yellow. Ice the tops of the cakes with yellow icing. Place the light red icing in a small pastry bag. Pipe small flower and dots on iced cakes.

# Dreams Come True Mini Pumpkin Muffins

With enchanted assistance from her Fairy Godmother, Cinderella arrives in a pumpkin-turned-carriage at the grand ball, where she waltzes with Prince Charming and wins his heart. After Cinderella flees the ball, Prince Charming seeks and finds her. Then it's wedding bells and fairytale endings. Although these mini pumpkin-and-spice muffins won't take you for a ride, they are mighty dreamy.

## Makes 24 mini muffins

1 cup all-purpose flour

1½ teaspoons baking powder

1½ teaspoons pumpkin pie spice

¼ teaspoon salt

1 large egg

½ cup packed light brown sugar

½ cup milk

½ cup pumpkin puree

2 tablespoons vegetable oil

½ teaspoon vanilla extract

Coarse sugar

Preheat the oven to 400°F. Line a 24-cup mini muffin pan with liners.

In a large bowl, sift together the flour, baking powder, pumpkin pie spice, and salt. Set aside.

In a medium bowl, whisk together the egg and brown sugar until well combined. Add the milk, pumpkin puree, oil, and vanilla extract. Whisk thoroughly to combine. Add the flour mixture to the egg mixture and stir until combined. Divide the batter evenly among the muffin cups. Sprinkle with coarse sugar, as desired. Bake for 14 to 16 minutes, or until lightly browned and cooked through (a toothpick inserted into the center of the muffins should come out clean).

Remove the mini muffins from the pan to a wire cooling rack. Serve warm or chilled.

# Jasmine Pistachio–Rosewater–Rice Cookies

Jasmine is compassionate and caring, unafraid to stand up for what's right. She's proud of her culture and a true leader, willing to enact change when necessary. And she knows when it's time to sit back and enjoy a sweet treat. Here's the treat that a princess like Jasmine would reach for: Persian rice cookies, traditionally called nan-e berenji—delicate, crumbly, light, and floral-flavor cookies.

## Makes about 18 cookies

- 4 tablespoons unsalted butter, melted
- ½ cup confectioners' sugar
- 1 egg yolk
- 1 tablespoon rosewater
- 1 cup rice flour
- ¼ teaspoon cardamom
- 1 tablespoon finely chopped pistachios

In a medium bowl, whisk together the butter and confectioners' sugar until glossy, about 1 minute. Add the egg yolk and rosewater, and whisk well to combine. Add the flour and cardamom, and stir well to combine. Cover the dough and chill in the refrigerator at least 6 hours to set the dough and allow the flavors to mingle.

Preheat the oven to 350°F. Line a large baking sheet with parchment paper.

Break off pieces of chilled dough and roll into ¾-inch balls. (If dough is stiff or crumbly, add a few drops of water at a time until slightly softened.)

Flatten balls slightly between your palms then place them on the baking sheet as close as ½ inch apart (these cookies spread very little). With the tip of a knife, cut a shallow X in the top of each cookie. Sprinkle cookies with pistachios. Bake for 18 to 20 minutes, or until cookies look dry but are not browned. Transfer cookies to a wire rack to cool. Store cookies in an airtight container at room temperature up to 5 days.

# Flynn Rider Blondie Bites

Because of her beautiful blonde hair, Flynn Rider calls Rapunzel "Blondie" when he first meets her. Rapunzel has good company with her sweet nickname. Another blondie is this type of buttery cookie bar, dotted with white chocolate chips.

## Makes 16 blondie bites

- ½ cup unsalted butter, melted
- 1 cup packed light brown sugar
- 1 large egg, beaten
- 1½ teaspoons vanilla extract
- 1 cup all-purpose flour
- ½ teaspoon baking powder
- ¼ teaspoon salt
- ½ cup white chocolate chips

Preheat the oven to 350°F.

In a large mixing bowl, stir together the butter and sugar. Add the egg and vanilla, then stir to combine. Add the flour, baking powder, and salt; stir again just until combined. Fold in the white chocolate chips.

Pour batter into an 8-inch-square glass baking dish. Spread batter with a spatula, or gently tap pan on countertop to evenly distribute batter.

Bake for 25 to 30 minutes, or until golden brown and dry on top. Remove blondies from oven. Cool on a wire rack at least 10 minutes. For uniform bars, cool completely, then cut into 16 squares. Store bars in an airtight container at room temperature up to 1 week.

# The Queen Applesauce Teacake

Disguised as an old woman, the Queen tricks Snow White with a poisoned apple, sending her into a deep slumber. Don't let that nasty trick with an apple prevent you from making and serving this delicate applesauce teacake. The confectioners' sugar finish asserts this cake to be the fairest of them all.

## Makes 8 to 10 servings

½ cup unsalted butter, softened, plus more for greasing

½ cup granulated sugar

½ cup packed light brown sugar

1 large egg

1 teaspoon vanilla extract

1 cup all-purpose flour

1 teaspoon baking soda

1 teaspoon ground cinnamon

½ teaspoon ground nutmeg

½ teaspoon salt

1 cup unsweetened applesauce

¼ cup confectioners' sugar

Preheat the oven to 400°F. Grease the sides and bottom of an 8-inch round cake pan with butter.

In a large bowl, cream together the butter, granulated sugar, and brown sugar with a mixer on medium. Add the egg and vanilla to the bowl, and beat well to combine.

In a medium bowl, sift together the flour, baking soda, cinnamon, nutmeg, and salt. With the mixer running on its lowest speed, add the flour mixture a little at a time until fully blended. Add the applesauce to the bowl and mix well to combine. Pour the batter into the prepared pan, and spread it into an even layer. Bake for 25 to 30 minutes, or until a toothpick inserted into the center comes out clean.

Remove the teacake from the oven. Cool for 20 minutes, and then loosen the edges of the cake from the pan with a knife. Turn the cake out onto a wire rack and then right the cake. Cool completely, about 1 hour.

Just before serving, dust the cake all over the top with confectioners' sugar. To do this, place the confectioners' sugar in a fine-mesh sieve and tap gently to release the sugar. (If you'd like, place a round wire cooling rack on the cake to act as a stencil to create a pattern of concentric circles.)

Leftovers should be stored at room temperature in an airtight container. The confectioners' sugar will melt into the cake after a day or so, but the cake is still good for 3 to 4 days.

# Fairy Godmother Sugar Cookie Wands

Cinderella's Fairy Godmother uses a magic wand to transform mice into coachmen and a horse into a driver, ensuring that Cinderella's dream of attending the royal ball comes true. How will you use your magic wand? You and your tea party guests can find out with these fun decorated cookie wands. You'll need 28 cookie sticks, which can be purchased in the baking section of crafts stores and large retail outlets.

## Makes about 28 cookie wands

### For the cookies

1½ cups confectioners' sugar

1 cup unsalted butter, at room temperature

2½ cups all-purpose flour

2 teaspoons baking powder

2 teaspoons vanilla extract

1 large egg

1 batch royal icing

### For the royal icing

2 cups confectioners' sugar

2 tablespoons warm water

1½ tablespoons meringue powder

Light blue and gold decorating sugars

**To make the cookies:** In a large bowl or the bowl of a stand mixer, combine the confectioners' sugar and butter. If using a large bowl, use a handheld mixer to beat the sugar and butter together on low speed. If using a stand mixer, use the paddle attachment. Add the flour and baking powder to the bowl, and mix again on low speed until fully incorporated. Cover the bowl with a lid, waxed paper, plastic wrap, or aluminum foil; chill in the refrigerator for at least 2 hours.

Remove the bowl from the refrigerator and preheat the oven to 375°F. Line a large baking sheet with parchment paper.

On a floured board, roll out one quarter of the dough at a time to ¼-inch thickness (cover and chill remaining dough until needed). Cut out dough with a 4-inch star-shape cookie cutter. Arrange stars on prepared baking sheet. For each wand, lightly insert one end of a cookie stick into a star.

If you are cooking in batches, chill the dough between batches.

Bake 8 to 10 minutes,or until just golden brown at the edges. Remove the cookies from the oven, and carefully transfer them with a spatula to a wire rack. Do not pick them up by the stick while hot; it will come out (if this happens, press it back in and let cool completely—it should reattach). Cool completely, at least 1 hour.

**To make the royal icing:** In a small bowl combine the confectioners' sugar, the water, and meringue powder. Beat on low speed until soft peaks form, 4 to 5 minutes. If icing is too thick or for thinner icing, add 1 to 2 teaspoons of additional water while beating.

Frost the cookies, then sprinkle on alternating stripes of light blue and gold decorating sugars.

CHAPTER 4

# Tiny Sandwiches and Soups

# Rapunzel Favorite Hazelnut Soup

Mother Gothel sets off to find the ingredients for Hazelnut Soup—Rapunzel's favorite—to celebrate Rapunzel's birthday. Inspired by that yummy soup, this rich, hearty version hits all the right notes of savory and herbal with a hint of sweetness, just right for a princess in a tower—or served in small portions for your tea time.

## Makes 4 servings

3 tablespoons olive oil

1 large onion, diced

4 cloves garlic, minced

1 teaspoon dried rosemary

1 apple, peeled and diced

1 pound parsnips, peeled and diced

¾ cup roasted hazelnuts, hulls removed, plus more for garnish

4 cups vegetable stock

½ teaspoon salt

¼ teaspoon black pepper

Fresh parsley, for serving

Heat the olive oil in a Dutch oven or heavy-bottom pot over medium heat. Add the onion and sauté until golden, about 5 to 7 minutes. Add the garlic, rosemary, apple, and parsnips, and cook, stirring, for 4 minutes. Add the hazelnuts, vegetable stock, salt, and pepper. Cover and bring to a boil. Then reduce the heat to low and cook for 20 to 25 minutes, or until the vegetables are tender. Remove the pot from heat and let cool slightly, about 10 minutes. The soup should have stopped boiling and sit for several minutes after to lose some of the heat. Then, using an immersion blender or a full-size blender, puree the soup. But be careful—hot soup can scald.

Divide the soup equally among four bowls. Serve the soup topped with additional hazelnuts and rosemary or a sprinkle of parsley.

# Cinderella Pumpkin Coach Soup

At the stroke of midnight, Cinderella's elegant carriage and stately coachman return to their previous forms of pumpkin and horse. Here's how to transform a pumpkin into soup, rather than a carriage. For tea time, serve the pumpkin soup in petite bowls; for a hearty lunch, serve in soup bowls.

## Makes 4 servings

1 tablespoon olive oil

1 small onion, diced

1 clove garlic, minced

2 cups vegetable broth

1 (15-ounce) can pumpkin puree

½ teaspoon dried sage

½ teaspoon dried rosemary

½ teaspoon paprika

¼ to ½ teaspoon salt

⅛ to ¼ teaspoon freshly ground black pepper

¼ cup pepitas

Heat the olive oil in a heavy-bottom large saucepan or small pot over medium heat. Add the onion and cook, stirring occasionally, until softened and golden brown, about 10 minutes. Add the garlic and cook for about 1 minute, until fragrant. Stir in the broth, puree, sage, rosemary, paprika, salt, and pepper. Cover the pot and bring to a boil. Reduce the heat to low and simmer the soup for 30 minutes. Stir well. Sprinkle with pepitas just before serving.

# Snow White German Potato Soup

The Seven Dwarfs return home from a full day's work to discover Snow White standing at the stove, stirring something in a heavy pot. "Smells good," exclaims Happy. What do you suppose Snow White has bubbling at the stove? Could it be this hearty German potato soup, made with leeks, bacon, onions, garlic, potatoes, and carrots?

## Makes 4 servings

1 large leek

4 ounces bacon, chopped

1 medium onion, diced

1 clove garlic, minced

1 pound russet potatoes, cut into ½-inch cubes

2 carrots, diced

3 cups chicken broth

Bay leaf

Salt and black pepper

To prepare the leek, remove the root end and then cut the bulb in half lengthwise. Then cut it into ¼-inch slices. Transfer the slices to a bowl of water, swish around to remove dirt, and let stand.

In a heavy-bottom pot or Dutch oven, cook the bacon, stirring occasionally, over medium-high heat until browned, 5 to 7 minutes. Use a slotted spoon to remove the bacon from the pan and set aside. Drain the leeks and add them to the pan along with the onion and garlic. Sauté for 5 to 7 minutes, or until softened. Add the potatoes, carrots, broth, bay leaf, salt, and pepper. Cover and cook over medium heat for 20 to 25 minutes, or until the potatoes and carrots are softened. Stir in the bacon. Season with to taste with salt and pepper.

# Merida Roast Turkey Finger Sandwiches

Merida and her family gather around an abundantly filled dinner table of sausages, potatoes, beef, roasted carrots, and juicy roasted turkey legs when they dine at the castle. For dainty tea party fare, however, these sandwiches of deli-sliced turkey will satisfy even hungry princes and princesses.

## Makes 12 sandwiches

- 1 (16-ounce) package attached soft dinner rolls
- ½ pound deli turkey, thinly sliced
- ¼ pound deli provolone cheese, thinly sliced
- 3 tablespoons unsalted butter, divided
- ½ teaspoon paprika
- ½ teaspoon oregano
- ½ teaspoon salt
- ¼ teaspoon black pepper

Preheat the oven to 350°F. Line a baking sheet with foil.

Slice the entire unit of rolls in half horizontally, keeping bottom and top of roll unit connected. Place the bottom portion of rolls on the backing sheet (top may extend slightly off sheet). Evenly divide turkey and cheese along bottom half of rolls.

In a small microwave-safe bowl, melt 2 tablespoons of the butter in the microwave. Stir in the paprika, oregano, salt, and pepper. Brush the butter mixture on the cut side of the roll tops. Replace the roll tops to cover the turkey and cheese layer.

Melt the remaining butter and brush on the assembled sandwiches. Bake 13 to 15 minutes, or until the rolls begin to brown. Remove the sandwiches from the oven, cool slightly, and then cut the rolls apart.

# Magic Carpet Toasts

Magic Carpet, the flying rug with a big, expressive personality, becomes Aladdin's friend in the Cave of Wonders. You, too, can be expressive by arranging toppings on "carpet" toasts; first spread with a blend of pistachios, mint, and creamy beans.

*Makes 8 toasts*

## For the bean spread

1 (15.5-ounce) can cannellini beans, drained and rinsed

1 clove garlic

1 tablespoon tahini

2 tablespoons pistachios

1 tablespoon chopped fresh mint

¼ teaspoon salt

¼ cup olive oil

4 slices bread, toasted

## Toppings

(At least 2 tablespoons of each, plus more as desired)

Chopped fresh mint

Chopped roasted red peppers

Chopped pistachios

Crumbled feta cheese

**To make the bean spread:** Combine the beans, garlic, tahini, pistachios, mint, and salt in a food processor or blender. Pulse or process on medium speed until evenly chopped. Drizzle in the olive oil and process until smooth, about 1 minute.

Remove the crusts from the bread, and cut each slice into 2 rectangles. Serve with the bean spread and small bowls of toppings, allowing each guest to design their own magic carpet.

# Golden Sun Egg Salad Tea Sandwiches

With a single drop of sunlight, a magical flower grew that healed the queen when she was pregnant. It was that flower cure that imbued baby Rapunzel with enchanted hair. Her hair glows golden when she sings a special song, healing the sick and giving youth to the old. But that's not all: Rapunzel finds so many uses for her very, very long hair—including using it as a lasso to lower herself to the ground. These sun-sational tea sandwiches, filled with creamy egg salad, are inspired by the golden sun that gave Rapunzel her magical hair.

## Makes 8 sandwiches

6 hard-cooked eggs, peeled
¼ to ⅓ cup mayonnaise
1 teaspoon ground mustard
Salt and black pepper
1 loaf soft sandwich bread

Cut the eggs into quarters and add them to a large bowl. Use a potato masher or the tines of a fork to partially mash the eggs. Add the mayonnaise, mustard, and salt and pepper to taste to the bowl. Stir well to combine, and adjust the seasonings as desired. Set aside.

Use a 2½- to 3-inch sun-shape cookie cutter to cut 1 to 2 sun shapes from 1 bread slice, depending on size of bread. Spoon egg salad onto half of the suns and top with the other half. Serve immediately.

# Captain Li Shang Pepper Jack Finger Sandwiches

Captain Li Shang, given the task to train Mulan and the new recruits, is logical, tough, determined, and loyal. He has a fiery strength to him as well, and so do these sandwiches, filled with sweet apricot jam and spicy pepper Jack cheese.

### Makes 8 sandwiches

8 thin slices white bread
½ cup apricot jam
¼ pound roast beef
4 slices pepper Jack cheese

On a cutting board, lay 4 of the bread slices. Spread each with jam.

Top jam with roast beef, cheese, and remaining 4 bread slices.

Use a serrated knife to cut crusts from sandwiches. Cut each in half, forming 8 sandwiches. Serve or chill until ready to eat.

# Evening Star Avocado Grilled Cheese

Tiana's firefly friend, Ray, is head over heels in love with Evangeline, the Evening Star that Tiana and others wish upon, hoping their dreams come true. These melty star-studded sandwiches, filled with avocado and sharp cheddar cheese, are a tribute to Evangeline.

## Makes 8 small sandwiches

8 thin slices firm bread (such as Pepperidge Farm Very Thin Enriched White Bread)

¼ cup unsalted butter, at room temperature, plus more for the skillet

1 avocado, peeled, pitted, and sliced

Salt and freshly ground black pepper

8 slices sharp cheddar cheese

Using a 1-inch star-shape cutter, cut 2 stars from 4 of the bread slices. Discard the cut-out star pieces. Butter one side of each of the 8 pieces of bread.

Heat a skillet over medium heat. Add a dollop of butter to the skillet to melt.

Meanwhile, in a small bowl mash together the avocado with a pinch each of salt and pepper. Divide the avocado evenly among uncut four slices of bread. Arrange two slices of bread, avocado-side up, in the skillet. Top each with 2 slices of cheese and the cut bread, with the buttered side facing up. Cook, turning once, until browned on both sides, 5 to 6 minutes total. Remove sandwiches from the pan and keep warm while cooking remaining sandwiches.

Cut the sandwiches in half to serve.

# Moana Toasted Coconut–Banana Toast

When the coconut grove on Moana's home island of Motunui is in trouble, Moana takes action. She goes on a brave journey to restore balance. Coconuts, like so much on the island, are very important to the residents of Motunui. Toasted with caramelized bananas, they are also important to these sweet open-face sandwiches.

## Makes 8 toast halves

4 slices whole wheat bread, toasted

¼ cup creamy peanut butter

2 medium almost-ripe bananas, cut into ½-inch-thick slices

2 tablespoons packed light brown sugar

1 teaspoon lemon juice

2 tablespoons butter

½ cup sweetened coconut

Thinly spread each toast with peanut butter; set aside.

In a medium bowl, stir together the banana slices, sugar, and lemon juice.

Heat the butter in a medium-size skillet over medium heat. Add the banana mixture and cook 3 to 4 minutes, until saucy and golden and bananas are softened yet hold their shape. Remove from heat and divide the mixture evenly on toasts.

In a small dry skillet over medium heat, stir and toast the coconut for 2 to 3 minutes, until golden brown. Sprinkle onto toasts. Cut toasts in half to serve.

# Be Our Guest Ham-and-Butter Baguette Bites

Won't you be our guest? That's what Lumiere, Mrs. Potts, Chip, and the rest of the staff sing as they dance around Belle, while she watches in awe. Wouldn't it be lovely if the staff also offered delightful bites, such as these open-face sandwiches, to their newly arrived guest? These bites are a version of a French favorite: jambon-beurre—a ham and butter sandwich.

## Makes about 20 baguette bites

- 1 French bread baguette, halved lengthwise
- 6 tablespoons salted butter, at room temperature
- 8 ounces sliced ham
- 1 tablespoon chopped fresh parsley

Butter the cut sides of each baguette half. Cut each baguette half into 2-inch-wide slices and place on a platter or cutting board for serving.

In a medium skillet over medium heat, cook the ham for 2 to 3 minutes per side until heated through. Layer ham on baguette slices, sprinkle with parsley, and serve.

CHAPTER 5

# Tea Party Sips

# Moana Coconut–Mango Coolers

Feel as daring as Moana while sipping on refreshing coconut-mango coolers during a tea party. Combine refreshing coconut water with sweet mango, tart lime, and bubbly club soda for a delightful drink.

*Makes four 7- to 8-ounce drinks*

2 cups coconut water

Juice from 1 lime

2 cups frozen mango

1 cup club soda, divided

Lime slices, halved, for garnish

In a blender, combine coconut water, lime juice, and frozen mango chunks. Blend until smooth. Divide blended mixture among four large beverage glasses. Top each with ¼ cup club soda. Serve immediately, garnished with lime slices.

# Belle Enchanted Rosewater Lemonade

The Beast has been cursed to find true love before the last petal falls from his enchanted rose. If he doesn't succeed, the beautiful rose, left by the enchantress, will fade, and as a consequence, the Beast and his friends will remain as they are. In this lemonade, floral rosewater is a reminder of the Beast's journey to understand love.

## Makes four 10-ounce drinks

### For the simple syrup

1 cup water

1 cup granulated sugar

1 tablespoon rosewater

### For the lemonade

3 cups water

Juice from 4 lemons (about ¾ cup)

Ice, for serving

Fresh mint, for garnish

**To make the simple syrup:** In a small saucepan combine the water, sugar, and rosewater. Heat and stir over medium heat until the sugar is dissolved, 2 to 3 minutes. Remove from heat.

**To make the lemonade:** Combine the water and lemon juice in a large pitcher. Stir in the simple syrup to combine. Chill until ready to serve. To serve, pour over ice and garnish with fresh mint.

# Snow White Warm Apple Cider

The Queen is so determined to be the fairest in the land that she attempts to replace Snow White once and for all with a poisoned apple. Thankfully, the Queen fails, and Snow White goes on to live happily ever after with the prince. Apples have so many good uses that it's hard to think of them in evil hands. This beverage is just one example of the goodness of apples.

*Makes eight 8-ounce servings*

½ gallon apple cider

½ orange, cut into slices

4 cinnamon sticks

1 teaspoon whole cloves

Pinch ground nutmeg

Cinnamon sticks and thinly sliced apple, for garnish

In a large pot, stir together the apple cider, orange slices, the 4 cinnamon sticks, the cloves, and nutmeg. Heat over low heat, covered, for 1 hour. Remove the orange slices and cinnamon sticks.

Serve in mugs, garnished with cinnamon sticks and thinly sliced apples.

# Cinderella Pumpkin-Spice Hot Cocoa

Oh, Cinderelly, Cinderelly! Cinderella's mouse friends sing about the many chores that Cinderella must do each day at the bidding of her stepmother and stepsisters. The friends, worried that Cinderella will have no time to sew a beautiful gown for the ball, stitch one as a gift. However, the jealous stepsisters rip the gown apart. Like Jaques and Gus Gus saving the day by helping Cinderella with her dress, pumpkin-spice hot cocoa sets the world—or at least the day—to all things right for tea party guests.

## Makes four 10-ounce servings

⅓ cup cocoa powder

½ cup packed dark brown sugar

1 teaspoon pumpkin pie spice

Pinch salt

⅓ cup water

4 cups milk

Mini marshmallows, for garnish

In a large saucepan, combine the cocoa powder, dark brown sugar, pumpkin pie spice, salt, and the water. Set the heat to medium and bring to a boil, stirring constantly. Once the sugar is dissolved, stir in the milk and heat thoroughly but not to boiling. Remove the cocoa from heat and divide evenly among four mugs.

Garnish with mini marshmallows.

# Mulan Iced Orange Green Tea

When Mulan meets with the matchmaker, she tells Mulan that she needs to exhibit dignity, refinement, and poise as she pours tea to please her future in-laws. The visit doesn't go well and the matchmaker is not impressed. Fortunately, Mulan finds her own path that brings her family honor. This refreshing iced tea with orange flavor is made with green tea. Though it's inspired by Mulan's unsuccessful experience with the matchmaker, this iced tea is definitely a success.

## Makes four 12-ounce servings

- 4 green tea teabags
- 4 cups boiling water
- 2 tablespoons honey
- Juice from 2 oranges (about 1 cup)
- 1 orange, cut into thin slices (ends discarded)
- Ice, for serving
- Fresh mint, for garnish

Place the tea bags into a large measuring cup or 4-cup heat-safe container. Add the boiling water and stir in the honey. Let steep, uncovered, for 10 minutes. Remove the teabags, pressing them with a spoon against the side of the container to extract all the green tea. Let cool at least 20 minutes.

In a pitcher, stir together the green tea and orange juice. Add the orange slices. Chill until ready to serve; serve over ice, garnished with fresh mint.

# Toast to the Future Sparkling Punch

Once a kiss from Aurora's true love, Prince Phillip, lifts Maleficent's evil curse, the kingdom awakens to celebrate. This colorful, flavorful, sparkling punch combines strawberry slush, ginger ale, and sherbet as the ideal drink to celebrate a happy ending and toast to the future.

## Makes four 14-ounce servings

2 cups frozen strawberries, partially defrosted

4 cups cold ginger ale

1 cup rainbow sherbet

In a food processor or blender, process the strawberries until smooth (strawberries may appear slushy). Divide the processed strawberries evenly among four 1-pint glasses. Slowly pour 1 cup of the ginger ale into each glass, pausing when bubbles rise.

Drop a ¼-cup scoop of sherbet into each glass. Serve with straws. Advise guests to stir gently before drinking to combine the flavors.

# Rapunzel Fruit Tea

While growing up locked in the tower, Rapunzel becomes creative in the kitchen—baking pies, dozens of cookies, and other sweet treats. Still, even as she experiments, she wonders when her real life will begin. This flavor-bending combination of fresh fruit juice and fragrant green tea would likely set Rapunzel to dreaming beyond the tower walls.

## Makes six 8-ounce drinks

2 cups watermelon

1 cup strawberries, plus more for garnish

½ cup blueberries

3 cups water, divided

3 green tea teabags

In a blender, combine the watermelon, the 1 cup strawberries, and the blueberries, and blend until smooth. Strain the mixture through a fine-mesh sieve into a pitcher, removing fruit solids. Stir in 1 cup of the water.

In a small pot, heat the remaining 2 cups water to boiling. Remove from heat and submerge the teabags in the hot water. Steep for 10 minutes, uncovered. Remove the teabags, then pour the tea into the punch. Stir to combine. Chill until ready to serve, or serve immediately over ice, garnished with fresh whole strawberries.

# Under the Sea Pineapple Punch

Sebastian is certain that life is better under the sea, although Ariel remains curious and embarks on an adventure of discovery. Even though Ariel finds love on solid ground, she'd surely appreciate this fruity, citrusy punch inspired by the colorful world on the ocean floor.

*Makes six 8-ounce drinks*

**For the simple syrup**

Zest from 2 limes

¼ cup water

¼ cup sugar

**For the punch**

Juice from 2 limes

1 cup water

3 cups pineapple juice

1 cup fresh pineapple chunks

1 cup raspberries

Pineapple spears, for garnish

**To make the simple syrup:** In a small saucepan, combine the lime zest, the ¼ cup water, and the sugar. Heat and stir over medium heat until the sugar dissolves. Remove the saucepan from heat.

**To make the punch:** In a large pitcher, combine the lime juice, the 1 cup water, and the pineapple juice. Drizzle in the simple syrup and stir to combine. Stir the pineapple chunks and raspberries into the punch. Chill at least 30 minutes before serving garnished with pineapple spears.

# Tiana Mardi Gras Smoothie

When Tiana and Naveen find their way back to New Orleans, they're caught up in the colorful Mardi Gras parade. Inspired by the bright colors of Mardi Gras, this smoothie is topped with colorful sprinkles. The smoothie ingredients are a take on King Cake, a traditional dessert served during Mardi Gras.

**Makes four 10-ounce smoothies**

2 cups milk

2 cups vanilla yogurt

2 tablespoons light brown sugar

⅔ cup pecans

½ cup golden raisins

Sanding sugar in purple, green, and gold

In a blender, combine the milk, yogurt, brown sugar, pecans, and raisins. Blend thoroughly until the pecans and raisins are itty-bitty pieces. Divide among 4 glasses. Decorate each with purple, green, and gold sugars, then serve.

# Palace Orange Blossom Chamomile Tea

Princess Jasmine lives with her father, the Sultan, in a grand palace. If Jasmine were looking for a delicious tea to share with her father, this would be the recipe. This sweetened, fragrant tea with orange blossom water is a wonderful sipper for any tea party.

**Makes four 8-ounce drinks**

4 chamomile teabags

¼ cup honey

1 tablespoon orange blossom water

4 cups water

Orange slices, for garnish

In a decorative teapot, place the teabags, honey, and orange blossom water. In a tea kettle or saucepan, bring the water to a boil, remove from heat, then fill the teapot. Cover and let steep for 10 minutes. Pour tea into 4 teacups or mugs.

Garnish with orange slices.

**Recipe Tip**

For a less sweet tea, reduce honey to 2 tablespoons.

# *Index*

PO Box 3088
San Rafael, CA 94912
www.insighteditions.com

Find us on Facebook: www.facebook.com/InsightEditions
Follow us on Twitter: @insighteditions

Disney

Library of Congress Cataloging-in-Publication Data available.

ISBN: 978-1-64722-375-5

INSIGHT EDITIONS
**Publisher:** Raoul Goff
**VP of Licensing and Partnerships:** Vanessa Lopez
**VP of Creative:** Chrissy Kwasnik
**VP of Manufacturing:** Alix Nicholaeff
**Editorial Director:** Vicki Jaeger
**Editor:** Anna Wostenberg
**Production Editors:** Jennifer Bentham and Jan Neal
**Production Manager:** Sam Taylor
**Senior Production Manager, Subsidiary Rights:** Lina Palma

WATERBURY PUBLICATIONS, INC.
**Editorial Director:** Lisa Kingsley
**Creative Director:** Ken Carlson
**Associate Editor:** Tricia Bergman
**Associate Editor:** Maggie Glisan
**Associate Art Director:** Doug Samuelson
**Production Assistant:** Mindy Samuelson
**Photographer:** Ken Carlson
**Food Stylist:** Jennifer Peterson
**Food Stylist Assistant:** Catherine Fitzpatrick

ROOTS of PEACE    REPLANTED PAPER

Insight Editions, in association with Roots of Peace, will plant two trees for each tree used in the manufacturing of this book. Roots of Peace is an internationally renowned humanitarian organization dedicated to eradicating land mines worldwide and converting war-torn lands into productive farms and wildlife habitats. Roots of Peace will plant two million fruit and nut trees in Afghanistan and provide farmers there with the skills and support necessary for sustainable land use.

Manufactured in China by Insight Editions

10 9 8 7 6 5 4 3 2 1

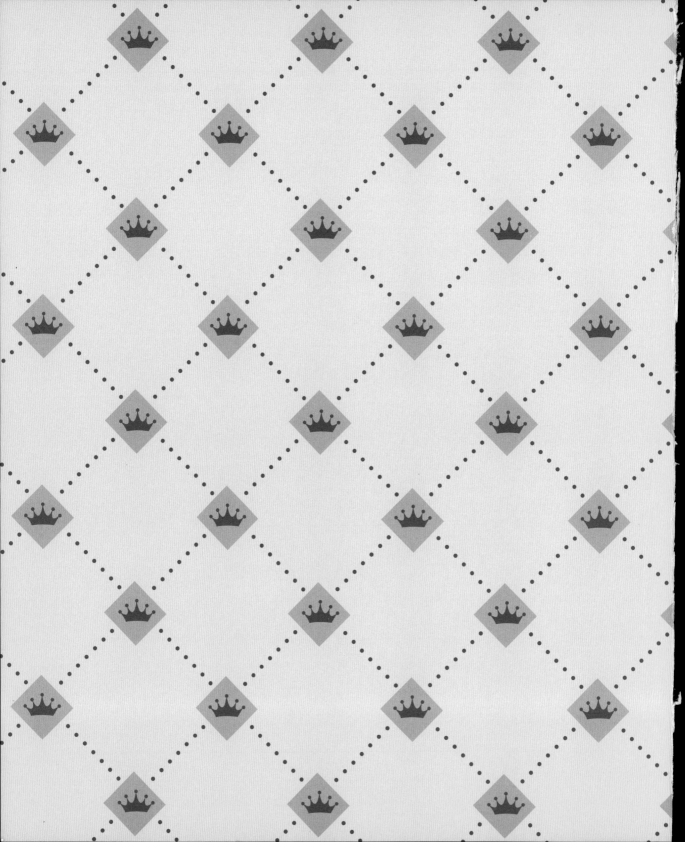